CHOSEN *by*
GOD

CHOSEN *by* GOD

*Learning Your Identity
and Position in Life*

FANELL E. WILLIAMS

purposely
created
PUBLISHING

CHOSEN BY GOD
Published by Purposely Created Publishing Group™
Copyright © 2019 Fanell E. Williams
All rights reserved.

Unless otherwise indicated, scripture quotations are from the Holy Bible, King James Version. All rights reserved.

Scriptures marked AMP are taken from the Amplified Version®. Copyright © 2015 by The Lockman Foundation. All rights reserved.

Printed in the United States of America

ISBN: 978-1-64484-103-7

Special discounts are available on bulk quantity purchases by book clubs, associations and special interest groups. For details email: sales@publishyourgift.com or call (888) 949-6228.

For information log on to www.PublishYourGift.com

I dedicate this book to my granny,
Jimester LittleAnn Daniel.

She always told me to "go on wit ya bad self"
and to shine brighter than the stars—how God
created me. I'm doing it, granny!

Table of Contents

Acknowledgments

I give ALL glory, honor, and praise to my Lord and Savior, Christ Jesus. Without God, this work would not have been possible. I know for a fact I would not be who and where I am today if it were not for His Holy Spirit. Thus far in my life, I have learned in depths from my past, am thankfully blessed for my present, and excited for my future!

I honor my mom, Paulina. She has been immensely supportive and understanding during my processes of deliverance, forgiveness, and healing. I love you dearly. I am grateful for my dad, Frank. Jesus is truly a loving, redemptive, and powerful savior. I love you so much.

I thank God for my aunt and pastor, Dr. Nadine R. Larde'. She has been there to push me through irritation, agitation, and frustration to the point of tears, which officially birthed me into ministry. I was unsure about writing this book but holding on to faith and using boldness has caused me to set myself aside and let God have His way. Thank God it is finally here!

I want to thank all those who I placed trust to proofread my first work. A very special moment!

And I would not omit you, the reader of my work. Thank you! It is my honor to present lessons I've learned through life experiences with hopes it aids you in whatever you may be going through or have gone through.

Foreword

It is an honor to be the aunt and pastor of Fanell E. Williams. I can testify of Fanell being an honest, very loving, and caring person. She has a way of touching the hearts of everyone she encounters. Fanell loves family and does her best at supporting and showing love and gratitude to all. Fanell is a great help when it comes to supporting and rendering her spiritual gifts and talents to the ministry. Everyone that I have spoken with concerning Fanell, I hear nothing but good reports. Fanell dives into the word of God at any opportunity that she gets, having a heart and desire to contain ministry. Fanell is always pursuing a deeper relationship with Christ. She is on the worship team and is the assistant administrator of Kingdom Inheritance. Fanell is awesome in movement ministry (worship dance). She is a psalmist and songwriter. She brings her gifts to the ministry and complements it. Fanell is a brain child. I was ecstatic when finding out Fanell had retained her master's in social work within a year. What an accomplishment! And speaking of accomplishments, whenever Fanell has a goal to reach, she always completes it.

Chosen by God: Learning Your Identity and Position in Life is an awesome work. Fanell E. Williams is a dynamic author who touches on and teaches how to identify your position when being challenged by the opposer. I would say, personally, the reading of Fanell's work is excellent, especially the part when she gives you three main reasons in depth concerning how the enemy does not like you, despises you, and hates you. *Chosen by God: Learning Your Identity and Position in Life* is a must read! Bravo, Fanell E. Williams. Bravo!

Dr. Nadine R. Larde'
Kingdom Inheritance, Senior Pastor

Introduction

Chosen by God: Learning Your Identity and Position in Life is a work that links the natural and the spiritual. It is a resource of learning and application. In this book you will find an introduction to my personal testimony with series to follow. I was guided by the Holy Spirit to write my unique story in parts as I continue my healing process. I have learned to conceal and protect those who have violated me in the past because just as I now have the opportunity to a new, positive life, they can too. Therefore, my story is not being shared for you to know, as people call, the "juicy details." It's all about forgiveness, because my purpose is to give you knowledge, understanding, and wisdom needed to capture and possess the keys to unlocking your own deliverance. This is my heart, "I will always remember to share my story for the glory of God."

The series that follows will provide keys to breaking generational curses and living a life of true liberty. I have for you generational curse breaking keys to use that include superimposition, which in my experience is when I relinquished all control to God, allowing Him to realign my life as He predestined. When I asked God to superimpose in my life (specifically in every area of my life), I gave up knowing the process of the who, what, when, why, where, and how. In this stage, you know that you alone cannot change your situation. A wilderness experience occurs when you must be alone for recalibration and you are definitely on your way to healing. Your life is about to change for the better. This process is needed for you to get to your total transformation or what I like to call your Life and Light Experience – being bound by nothing. Transformation is necessary for living a life of freedom. The transformation process will uncover what I call your *God-Given Identity and Position.* The only way to get there is with the guidance of the Holy Spirit.

I prophesy that the Holy Spirit is beginning to reinstate your true identity and position!

I am so excited to share more with you in my upcoming series about how God, all along, had a purpose for me. It has been a journey of uncertainty, agitation, and irritation but also change, growth, and a blossoming. As you continue to read, please try to keep in mind that what happened to you or what you have even done to someone is not your God-given identity. I say this because people have done so many inappropriate things to me, even loved ones. In turn, I found myself acting out the same. However, when one acknowledges, repents, and asks God for forgiveness, they will ultimately receive reconciliation, salvation, and the grace of God. These are a few of the main reasons I can share my story. Once I began to understand the natural and spiritual side of things, I was able to see everything from a different perspective, including the people involved.

And the journey begins.

In November 2017, I surrendered EVERYTHING to God, which released me from mental and spiritual captivity. I have been *completely* delivered, which is to bring and hand over to the proper recipient. Yes, I was returned from darkness handed to God the Father by the blood of Jesus. Now, that does not mean after deliverance I did not and do not face opposing forces. There are definitely challenges! However, as a result of my experiences, I have become resilient. This has molded me as a person to make conscious choices *every single day* to persevere forward. Nothing will stop me!

I can remember being exposed to sexual perversion as a young child. I have not been through all the following experiences. However, sexual perversion includes but is not limited to:

- What I call Early Sexual Exposure (ESE), which includes sexual grooming and molestation
- Fantasies
- Fetishes
- Homosexuality
- Incest
- Masturbation

- Etc.

You may ask, why would a young child have to go through these experiences? To answer that question, you should know that no one is exempt from experiencing some form of perversion. Perversion is not only sexual, but it is anything presented in a state of distortion or corruption. However, sexual perversion has its way of entering into someone's life during childhood whether it's exposure through television, a Playboy magazine, surfing the web, or spending the night at a friend's house.

Even if you have not had any of these experiences, I know that this book will help you with answers. It is my God-given privilege to offer help in enhancing your journey in the process of your deliverance, healing, and a guide to forgiveness. You will be able to live a life of freedom with the capabilities of making choices that honor peace and the wholesomeness you deserve in your life. By seeking a relationship with God, you will have the keys for living an abundant life. Seek God and see.

Natural and Spiritual

Genesis 2:5 (KJV)

*"...And every plant of the field before it was in the earth,
and every herb of the field before it grew: for the LORD
God had not caused it to rain upon the earth,
and there was not a man to till the ground."*

On October 28, 2018, I posted on Facebook: "This life is more than just natural. This life is more than just spiritual. This life is both. Pay attention to both." How do I know this life is natural and spiritual? I have experienced natural and spiritual things – some good, some bad. I went through over ten years of darkness that consisted of Early Sexual Exposure, trauma (neglect and loss), vulnerabilities being preyed upon, and boundaries being crossed. From firsthand experience, I know for a fact the enemy is strategic, attacking when a person is most vulnerable. This is what happened to me as a child. The Holy Spirit revealed to me that attacks from the enemy are attached to a person being ignorant as well.

I'm sure that if you have gone through any level of drama or trauma you've asked the same question I have.

"Why me?" In my experience with talking in general about people going through situations and asking this question, the most common response is, "Why not?" At first, this response sufficed to fulfill the void of not understanding why I had to go through a more than ten-year period in darkness. What I mean by darkness is captured best by Stephen R. Chestnut and I quote, "Darkness is not the absence of light. It is the absence of revelation." I wondered why I could display a sense of joy through smiling and laughing daily, even though privately I felt lost and a deep sense of sadness.

For a long time, because of my innocence and need to feel loved, I did not know that what was presented to me was inappropriate in its nature and timing. This condition was normal to me, but it wasn't right. It's important to understand that just because something is normal to you does not mean it is right. Normal is habitual, routine, or a cycle—something done repeatedly over a period of time. During this dark cycle, my God-given identity and position could not be revealed, was not being developed and cultivated, and definitely was not activated for me to operate in.

I prophesy every dark, negative, demonic cycle will begin to break in your life even now! I prophesy God's light. New, positive, blessed cycles will emerge in your life! It's time for the real you to arise!

So let me answer both questions for you as to the reasoning behind what you experienced. It is because *God has a purpose for you.* He can deliver you out of anything that forces you into bondage and makes you feel powerless. Your God-given birthright is to have dominion. Place your trust in Him. Your God-given identity—who you really are—and your God-given position—what you are really supposed to be doing—*is why.* We have been so accustomed to seeing with our natural eyes and paying attention to ONLY the natural side of things that what is seen is all that there is. No, No, NO! This is a lie, an illusion, a deception that the enemy runs with knowing we don't possess this knowledge. Hosea 4:6 (KJV) reads: *"My people are destroyed for lack of knowledge..."*

From this day forward, I prophesy, you will no longer walk in ignorance of the dual life we live.

In conjunction with providing information about the natural and spiritual, I cannot go without talking about our relationship with God in spirit before natural. I learned this while in service at my home church. The portion of scripture in Genesis 1:26-31 illustrates how God spoke and created man in His own image. It further reads how God blessed them and said who they are to be and what they are to have by instruction, and what God provided for them. When we go to the scripture Genesis 2:4-7, it talks about the **generations** of the heavens and of the earth God created. We read here the wording, *"And every plant of the field before it was in the earth..."*

In simple terms, God spoke what He was going to do first. He had an idea, observed, and then put His plan into action. Nothing was seen in the natural, nor was it seen to the physical eye yet because Genesis 1:2 (KJV) says, *"And the earth was without form, and void; and darkness was upon the face of the deep. And the Spirit of God moved upon the face of the waters."* This has to do with spiritual things, which is why the Spirit of God had to move upon the face of the waters. Water or some other type of life-supporting liquid is crucial because that is the avenue of how things are birthed. Through studying, you will find that water is symbolic for the Holy Spirit. As I stated in the introduction of this book: seek a relationship with God. Relationship comes through our encounters and experiences with God, and our exposure to the word of God.

Jeremiah 1:5 (AMP) says, *"Before I formed you in the womb I knew [and] approved of you [as My chosen instrument], and before you were born I separated and set you apart, consecrating you; [and] I appointed you as a prophet to the nations."* Now it is understood everyone is not a prophet and everyone is not called to the nations. However, when God spoke, He spoke to everything and everyone. Genesis 1:26 (AMP) says, *"God said, Let Us [Father, Son, and Holy Spirit] make mankind in Our image..."* When

God was speaking, He was speaking about all of His creation—even before we were here on earth. That "man" or "mankind" definitely includes you! God knew you before you were formed in your mother's womb. Were you physical then? No. Were you just invisible? No. Were you non-existent because you were not seen? No. Before we were born into this world, God formed us in His likeness and image for the purpose of dwelling on the earth. When we were with God, we were formless spirits before He created and formed us naturally. You are one out of literally millions that manifested. That is no coincidence!

God had a relationship with you before you were conceived in the womb and born into this world. Any creation had to come from a creator; first as an idea or concept (spirit, seen by vision), then it had to manifest (natural, seen by sight). Steve Jobs had a relationship with Apple before we knew about it. Bill Gates had a relationship with Microsoft before it was known to others. Dr. Patricia Bath had a relationship with the Laserphaco Probe, a tool that corrects cataracts during eye surgery, before it was known to others[1]. Otis Boykin had a relationship with the IBM computer and the pacemaker before we ever knew about them[2]. See the reoccurring theme? The creator had a relationship with

---

[1] https://www.makers.com/blog/8-black-female-inventors-who-will-inspire-you-think-big

[2] https://thinkgrowth.org/14-black-inventors-you-probably-didnt-know-about-3c0702cc63d2

the creation before it was known to others. "Relationship" is two or more individuals, their connection, and how they behave toward one another. This means, with God having a relationship with you before you were born...YOU also had a relationship with God.

Since the Book of Jeremiah is in the Old Testament portion of the Bible, we will look at what the word *knew* means in the Hebrew. *Knew* in the Hebrew means to be acquainted with[3]. Whether the creation remembers or not, the creator had an intimate relationship with the creation before the creation was even created. Read that again slower. Whether the creation remembers or not, the creator had an intimate relationship with the creation before the creation was even created. See, in Colossians 1:16-17 (AMP) it reads, "*For it was in Him that all things were created...all things were created and exist through Him [by His service, intervention] and in and for Him. And He Himself existed before all things, and in Him all things consist (cohere, are held together)."* Again, God had an intimate relationship with us as spirit beings before He created us as human beings.

---

3 https://itunes.apple.com/us/app/strongs-concordance-kjv-bible/
   id1113008391?mt=8

Reflective Journal

Think and write about the natural (what is seen by sight) and spiritual (what is seen by vision) in your life. In other words, what do you see further than your natural circumstances?

_____

_____

_____

_____

_____

_____

_____

_____

_____

_____

_____

_____

_____

_____

The Enemy

John 10:10 (AMP)

"The thief comes only in order to steal and kill and destroy. I came that they may have and enjoy life, and have it in abundance (to the full, till it overflows)."

What the Enemy Knows About You and What Deception He Uses Against You

Did you know that the enemy is a coward? His greatest attraction is to people he can attack when they're most vulnerable, susceptible, or defenseless. The enemy's ultimate goal is to attack and attach darkness to your identity. When the enemy comes to realize God has granted you your God-given identity and Kingdom position, he immediately takes offence and commences for an attack. You must keep in mind these three factors when it comes to the enemy trying to destroy your identity and prevent you from being in position:

1. The enemy does not like you – AT ALL.
2. The enemy wants to destroy you.
3. The enemy does not want your identity revealed or for you to fulfill your Kingdom purpose. He wants you to fail.

Enemy is defined as being hated, hateful, hostile, and opposing (God) in the mind. What stood out to me was the fifth definition. From the Greek definition of enemy – he's the ***most bitter*** and a great enemy of the divine government[4]. *Bitter* means one's behavior is hurt, resentful, and vengeful. John 10:10 (KJV) says, *"The thief cometh not, but for to steal, and to kill, and to destroy..."* You have heard of the saying, "Hurt people, hurt people." Well I believe the enemy "feels" like he has been treated unjustly. Because of his behavior, the enemy will be condemned to one miserable place for all eternity. In Revelation 20:10 (AMP) it reads, *"Then the devil who had led them astray [deceiving and seducing them] was hurled into the fiery lake of burning brimstone, where the beast and false prophet were; and they will be tormented day and night forever and ever (through the ages of the ages)."*

So I have a serious question for you. Why would Lucifer—described as perfect in beauty and being perfect in his ways from the day he was created until iniquity was found in him (Ezekiel 28:12,15)—not want you to be bitter with him? With all the hell you have gone through, know that if bitterness sits in your heart, it will fuel hate and hostility. Beware of becoming bitter from the bad you've experienced. With God, you can take the bad and convert it into better. Keep reading and you will learn how.

---

[4] https://itunes.apple.com/us/app/strongs-concordance-kjv-bible/id1113008391?mt=8

The enemy sends an attack of darkness and tries to attach it to you to cause you to lose or let go of your light. This causes you to lose the shining light of Christ. The enemy aims his attacks, especially towards the very young—even while the embryo is yet in the womb. This attack can be internal by the mother going through emotional or physical stress, the use of alcohol and drugs, bad or broken relationships, and emotional breakdown; all of these affect the body directly. Another attack may come from an external source like physical, emotional, or verbal abuse inflicted on the mother. As you are developing, you are most innocent. As a small child, you are susceptible to your environment, especially to the people who are responsible for you.

This is what I have learned over the years. If not internal, the next window of attack will be external, physically or mentally to that child, because all children's minds are like a sponge, absorbing everything. As a child, one soaks in everything they are exposed to whether good or bad. Children do not have the capability to defend themselves mentally, let alone physically. So now that we know when and why the enemy does this, I'm going to take the three factors I mentioned to you earlier and explain them more in depth.

The first factor is the enemy does not like you at all. The enemy actually despises you, and more than that he hates you. The word says in 2 Corinthians 11:14 (KJV), *"And no marvel; for Satan himself is transformed into an angel of light."* The enemy will do everything in his power to make what he presents to you look right for you, when, in reality, it is just the opposite. The enemy does this because he is jealous and envious of you in so many ways. One, we have a physical body and have been given instruction in Genesis to **BE** fruitful, multiply, have dominion, and subdue the Earth. We are made in the very image of God (Genesis 1:26).

The enemy is spirit and is able to present and influence us to be distracted from what God has for us. Secondly, we are able to repent, turn away from what we have done wrong, and resist it. The enemy, because of pride and wanting to be God, instead of staying in the position God created him to be in, was cast out of heaven with his angels (Revelation 12). This is why the enemy is bitter. The enemy would love to have possession over your body. *"Do you not know that your body is the temple (the very sanctuary) of the Holy Spirit Who lives within you, Whom you have received [as a Gift] from God?"* (1 Corinthians 6:19, AMP).

The second factor is the enemy ultimately wants to destroy you. We cannot afford to be ignorant when it comes to the enemy of our souls. Again, the bible says in John 10:10 (AMP), *"The thief comes only in order to steal and kill and destroy."* It is important to understand that Satan has a mission to steal, kill, and destroy you. Take time out and think on what it is that the enemy is trying to make you miss, abort, or stop you from doing. The enemy is not only trying to tempt you, distract you, and make you feel bad. These are only a means to an end. What is vital to your fight of faith is to know the result the enemy is after. The enemy's desires are to steal, kill, and destroy what's on the inside of you—your gifts, purpose, and relationship with God—to succeed in destroying YOU. Your God-given identity and position depend on your relationship with God. Acquire and protect it.

The third factor is the enemy does not want you to walk in your identity or fulfill your purpose. He wants you to fail. Make a declaration everyday as to **who** you are and **what** your purpose is, which is your Kingdom identity and position. If you don't have an answer say this prayer, "Dear Heavenly Father, I understand that you are my Creator. You have a purpose for my life and a Kingdom identity wherefore I must perform a work. So I'm asking you to lead and guide me with your precious Spirit and reveal to me who I am in you and the reason you have me here. In Jesus' name, Amen." If you don't ask yourself questions and seek to find the answers, you will continue to walk in darkness or repeat the same cycles not conducive for your life. This darkness or these cycles will diminish the life out of dreams you have or dreams to come. When you are in darkness, you don't know where you are going which results in repeated cycles. Get out of darkness and step into God's marvelous light (1 Peter 2:9)!

The enemy's temptations of distraction, disobedience, and fear are subtle strategies to eventually defeat you. What he has introduced to you during your younger years has conditioned your way of thinking, even using those closest to you. I mean, momma told me to not say anything and daddy wasn't there. From the cognition of a child, a situation seems to be a permanent condition when it is actually a temporary circumstance. As that child becomes an adult, that same way of thinking grows with them if they are not taught something different. But remember, the enemy is a deceiver, a liar, a falsifier, an illusionist, a manipulator, a ridiculer, an accuser, etc.

One thing the enemy does not want to do is scare you away. Let me repeat. One thing the enemy DOES NOT want to do is scare you away. He wants to lure you into the depths of darkness. When someone's intention is to distract you and destroy you, why would they let you know? Why would they warn you? When one has a hidden agenda, you will not know until it is exposed. Genesis 3:1 (AMP) says, *"NOW THE serpent was more subtle and crafty than any living creature of the field which the Lord God had made..."* The enemy is sensible, which means when he plans something, he does so cunningly. What he presents to you will be attractive, something you desire, something you want. Keep in mind he is an ancient demon who has been around for a long time. However, God is Alpha and Omega, the beginning and the ending. The Holy Spirit is a revealer, so what's in the dark will be exposed by the light (Luke 8:17). God won't leave you ignorant.

Reflective Journal

Think and write about the darkness that needs to be removed from your life in order for your light to shine.

_____

_____

_____

_____

_____

_____

_____

_____

_____

_____

_____

_____

_____

God-Given Identity and Position

1 Peter 2:9 (KJV)

"But ye are a chosen generation, a royal priesthood, an holy nation, a peculiar people; that ye should shew forth the praises of him who hath called you out of darkness into his marvelous light;"

Identity and Position

Your identity is what distinguishes you as an individual. Your position is the space you occupy. The definition that stood out to me the most of *position* is a set of circumstances, especially one that affects one's power to act. These definitions tell us God has created us with distinctiveness and put us in a position that gives us the advantage over our enemy. Genesis 1:26 says, *"And God said, Let us make man in our image, after our likeness: and let them have dominion..."* Innately, we have a position of authority. When we begin to understand and see ourselves this way, we can operate from a place of knowing instead of doubt.

Position Without Identity Is Impossible

When you don't know who you are, and you don't know your Godly status, you'll assume any position. One of the main ways a person will become knowledgeable and possess their God-given identity and position is in God. No matter your level of relationship with God, know that He is the one who created you. You did not place yourself here. You did not make it by chance. You were hand-picked, you were called, you were chosen by God. You have a purpose and the only way you can fulfill and walk in your purpose is when your God-given identity and position are revealed, activated, and obtained. We must learn who we are to know what we are supposed to perform.

Position Comes with Instruction

God made male and female in His image, after His likeness. He gave us specific benefits and instructions while we were yet spirit. God blessed us and instructed us to be fruitful, and multiply, and replenish the earth, and subdue it: and have dominion (Genesis 1:27-28). Understand that being fruitful and multiplying are commands that God has given us from the beginning. The word *fruitful* means to bear fruit, grow, or increase. The word *multiply* means to be or become great, enlarge, do much, or increase. God, our Creator, ordered and requires us to INCREASE. The question is, what will you increase in? Prayerfully after this read, you will increase in your God-given identity and position.

Who Are You Really?

God has already told you who you are. Who told you that you were any different? Who lied to you? Just as in the beginning with Adam and Eve in the garden (Genesis 3:11, AMP), they told God they were naked, and He asked them, *"Who told you that you were naked?"* There is only one who could shift the perception of a God-given position to a wrong condition. Adam and Eve were tricked to believe in an illusion, that something was wrong with their God-given identity, so they stopped standing in their dominion position. Since their eyes were opened (Genesis 3:7), their vision became natural sight – changing how they saw themselves. God formed man and made woman exactly how He wanted, and they were made in His image and likeness. The enemy distorted their perception, causing man to let go of their God-given identity and fall out of their Kingdom position. God does not want you to focus on your condition, but the position in Him and what He told you from the beginning, which is connected to your God-given identity.

A key deception of the enemy is to cause people to believe lies. He is the father of lies (John 8:44, AMP). The lie is what makes you see yourself different than how God has really made you. You may have been told you are not worthy, of value, or purpose. That is a lie. The result of a lie may be staying in perversion, in addiction, and disobedience to God. Again, the enemy wants the condition you are facing to overpower the position you are to assume. No, I'm not saying what you are going through and how you feel does not matter. You matter, but what I want you to understand is the condition you are in is for you to overcome so that you can arise with your Godly identity, obtain your Kingdom position, and begin to walk in your purpose.

See, woman was in the garden of Eden for a short time before the snake came to tempt her. Adam did name her, calling her Woman because she was taken out of Man (Genesis 2:23). The one critical missing piece was Adam did not inform the woman of her position with him. Adam knew who he was and was actually in position, dressing the garden and naming everything. The ultimate fall happened when the woman introduced the fruit to Adam, and he ate of it. The enemy not only wants to cause you to fall, but someone who is connected to you also.

This is why it is so vital for you to know your identity and be in the correct position. Knowing your identity and being in position is connected to someone else's identity and position. Don't forget this! The enemy was able to reach the woman at her most vulnerable state, causing her to be out of position to protect Adam. As a result of the woman being out of position, this caused Adam to fall, which affected the entire human race.

However, ALL things work together for the good to them that love God (Romans 8:28, KJV). Whatever happened to you is not your fault. Whatever you did wrong is not who you are. A person can be taunted and tormented by the enemy through their past or wrongdoings; this is called condemnation. In Romans 8:1 (KJV) it reads, *"There is therefore now no condemnation to them which are in*

Christ Jesus..." God has given you the ability to persevere and have the victory. You think things just happened to you by that family member, friend, or stranger because that is just life. A healthy mind realizes that overcoming circumstances and situations beyond their control gives God the privilege of transforming one's life and allowing their testimony to touch the lives of others.

People benefit from your yes, your obedience, your victory! Don't let a temporary circumstance determine who you are. Don't let what someone else says overpower what God has said about who you are and the rank you hold in Him. It's time for you to know your God-given identity and position!

Reflective Journal

Think and write about you at your best version. What
do you need to start doing today to get closer to
that vision of you? (mentally, emotionally, physically,
spiritually, etc.)

_____

_____

_____

_____

_____

_____

_____

_____

_____

_____

_____

_____

_____

Countdown for Transformation

It is vital for you to know who you are and what your purpose is in this life.

I remember a day in February when I and a couple other ladies were having a discussion about identity and destiny. This is a close example of what occurred. As we were talking, one of the young women said she didn't know who she was or what her purpose is. She felt lost. While others were comforting her, I sat and thought. *I need to know my purpose.* The reason I did not know is because I had just emerged from a lengthy, dark season of being a victim. During that time, I did not even realize my life was convoluted. See, when you're in darkness your judgement and perception about life is impaired.

Without spiritual awareness, you are more likely to take things at face value. Not knowing that there was an escape, I succumbed to the events happening in my life. It takes Christ to remove the scales off your eyes. Once the Lord removed the scales off of my eyes, I could recognize and see what truly transpired in my life. This is where revelation given by the Holy Spirit came into play. Not only did He deliver me from having a hardened heart, but He made in me a forgiving heart where I can now extend grace and learn how to love with healthy boundaries. I would describe my previous life as upside down, and Jesus turned it right side up. I have truly received a second chance.

I'll tell you, my heart was heavy. I wanted to help her but didn't know what to say. Then the Holy Spirit prompted me to open my heart and share parts of my testimony when deep inside, I felt insufficient. As others were trying to convince her that her life has purpose, she expressed with anguish, "It's hard. I'll just do what I've heard. I'll just fake it until I make it." I expressed to her through my experience to press while pursuing all while becoming. I told her to practice to become. The Holy Spirit revealed to me that the present is for practice in preparation for the future. If you don't practice *now* to become your best self, you won't ever become. In order to aim for your destiny, there must be an activation of faith in God. See, Jesus is the author and finisher of your faith (Hebrews 12:2). It is understood that "...faith is the substance of things hoped for, the evidence of things not seen" (Hebrews 11:1) and "...without faith it is impossible to please him..." (Hebrews 11:6). My suggestion to you is to find out who you are in Christ. Read 2 Corinthians 5:17 (KJV). It's time for your new!

Here's the Countdown for Transformation:

1. Repentance – sincere regret or remorse for the wrong one has done.

2. Deliverance – being rescued or set free. God will set you free from the bondage of hurt, anger, pain, bitterness, and so much more.

3. Forgiveness – the action of letting go of the wrong one has done. When you forgive others, God forgives you.

4. Healing – the process of becoming sound or healthy again.

5. Renewal – to be repaired from violation or damage.

6. Reconciliation – to be restored in Christ.

7. Transformation – a dramatic change in form, appearance, and within.

8. Purpose – why you are here, your God-given identity and position. WALK IN IT!

Everything you have read in this countdown will shift your life into a realm of continuous transformation through the power of the Holy Spirit. I guarantee. I'm doing it. You start it and see the results! I continue to walk in freedom and increase in my God-given identity and position every day. *"...press toward the mark for the prize of the high calling of God in Christ Jesus."* (Philippians 3:14, KJV)

Reflective Journal

Think and write about the areas in your life where you
need to repent and forgive. It's time to make way for your
transformation.

_____

_____

_____

_____

_____

_____

_____

_____

_____

_____

_____

_____

_____

Prayer and Purpose
Affirmations

At this point, I would love to pray for you. As I have prayed during my year's journey, I have learned to pray God's will; not my own. This prayer is with you in mind and written in love, peace, joy, and the Holy Spirit! Know that if something happened to you or you did something wrong, it does not take away your responsibility for your healing or justify your actions. This is just the first step in gaining insight on the spiritual along with your natural, beginning your journey with God, and aligning with His will for your life.

Prayer
Heavenly Father, thank you for the person reading this book. I am asking that you bring them peace which passes all understanding. Allow them to seek your Kingdom and your righteousness so that you will add unto them their identity and position in you. Let them find strength in you. Send your Holy Spirit to comfort them. Guide them through the trauma they may have faced and the chal-

lenges to come. Lord, bless the reader of this work with an increase of knowledge, understanding, and wisdom of the natural and spiritual. Jesus, enter into their hearts now and begin to do spiritual surgery to remove, heal, and mend every piece of their life that was broken, violated, abused, or misused. Begin to give them revelation, clarity, and understanding of their natural circumstances and the spiritual that they may be unaware. Let your love unharden their hearts so they can be delivered, so they can forgive, so they can be healed and whole. Become their strength in order for transformation to take place in their lives and give them the stamina to endure the changes and transitions to becoming who you have called them to be. Cancel, remove, and destroy worry, fear, and lack. Activate, put into place, and bring to life trust, boldness, and abundance! Your will be done. In the name of Jesus, Amen.

Purpose
Until it is engrained in your mind who God says you are, you need to say things that serve what God has said about you as often as possible. Every time the devil accuses you to be ashamed. Every time the enemy condemns you to curse you and the God who created you. Every time that shame silences you. Every time that depression presses you down. *Speak the truth that your creator has said to you and about you.*

Say aloud: I am God's! He died and shed His blood for me! He covers and is there for me! He won't put more on me than I can bear! I am the head and not the tail! I am fearfully and wonderfully made! Greater is He that is in me than he that is in the world! I am more than a conqueror and I can do all things through Christ which strengthens me! My latter will be greater than my former!

Say and repeat these statements (which means they are non-negotiable) until you know, mean, and believe them. Continue to add to these affirmations. When other thoughts or emotions that are contrary to what God has said comes in like a flood to your mind and body, know that God will raise up a standard (Isaiah 59:19, KJV). This is one of the best ways to triumph!

From my heart to yours, I believe in your victory. Know that God loved you so much that He gave His son Jesus to die on the cross for you that you might be saved and reconciled with God, our Creator. That word *loved* means before you were even born God loved you! Know that you are precious in God's eyes. He pays attention to you so closely that He knows the number of hairs on your head. You are His child. You, again, are so loved!

Reflective Journal

Think and write more purpose affirmations from scripture or other positive resources that you can say and repeat every day.

_____

_____

_____

_____

_____

_____

_____

_____

_____

_____

_____

_____

_____

About the Author

Fanell E. Williams, a licensed social worker, committed her life to being of service to others. Earning an associate's, bachelor's, and master's in social work, she is well trained in her passion for informing, empowering, and inspiring people toward their transformation. Her two nominations for the Ohio Liberator Award and earning the 2016 Social Justice Leader Award affirmed her motivation for helping people to heal and walk in freedom.

In addition to practicing social work, Fanell lives in her purpose through singing, speaking, worship dancing, volunteerism, and writing. For three years, she volunteered for the Lucas County's Human Trafficking and Trauma-Informed Care Coalitions. Her first book, *Chosen by God: Learning Your Identity and Position in Life*, is one of her many ventures in hopes of inspiring others to know their worth and live in their healing place through a variety of creative avenues. When she isn't serving others, Fanell enjoys reading, styling hair, listening to music, learning new things, and traveling.

To connect, email her at
fewministries19@gmail.com

CREATING DISTINCTIVE BOOKS
WITH INTENTIONAL RESULTS

We're a collaborative group of creative masterminds
with a mission to produce high-quality books to position
you for monumental success in the marketplace.

Our professional team of writers, editors, designers,
and marketing strategists work closely together to ensure
that every detail of your book is a clear representation
of the message in your writing.

Want to know more?
Write to us at info@publishyourgift.com
or call (888) 949-6228

Discover great books, exclusive offers, and more at
www.PublishYourGift.com

Connect with us on social media

@publishyourgift

CPSIA information can be obtained
at www.ICGtesting.com
Printed in the USA
BVHW081540230819
556656BV00007B/186/P